MICROWAVING WITH A GOURMET FLAIR

Published by:
Microwave "Helps"
P.O. Box 32223
Minneapolis, Minnesota
55432

MICROWAVING WITH A GOURMET FLAIR

Recipes by Joyce Battcher
Edited by Arlene Hamernik
Illustrations by Debora Novitsky

First Printing - February, 1978
Revised and Reprinted - March, 1979
Third Printing - August, 1979
Fourth Printing - November, 1980

Copyright © Microwave "Helps" - 1978

For permission to reproduce any part, address the publisher.

ISBN 0-9602930-1-9

DEAR FRIENDS,

MICROWAVING WITH A GOURMET FLAIR is combining the speed and many advantages of microwave cooking with the top-quality ingredients, classic ideas and sound basic principles of gourmet cooking.

MICROWAVING WITH A GOURMET FLAIR is truly creative cooking where we may adapt a classic recipe or gourmet-style recipe and cook it entirely by microwaves, prepare one or two parts of it by microwaves or reheat it by microwaves.

MICROWAVING WITH A GOURMET FLAIR is being excited about microwave cooking. It is experimenting with our microwave ovens to cook a variety of foods in a variety of styles.

MICROWAVING WITH A GOURMET FLAIR is easy, but it is not nonchalent cooking. We still need to stir and rearrange foods and, in some cases, rotate dishes or be very attentive for a few minutes of alternately microwaving and stirring. As in conventional cooking, we must plan ahead, read recipes through, have ingredients and equipment ready and use good judgement in timing, seasoning and in testing doneness.

MICROWAVING WITH A GOURMET FLAIR is this recipe booklet that includes variations of some classic recipes or ideas and many original recipes.

Most of the recipes are easy to prepare, but some take extra patience or attention for perfect results. Some may appear long and complicated, but they are written in detail to minimize problems or failures.

I hope your enthusiasm for MICROWAVING WITH A GOURMET FLAIR will continue to grow as you use the recipes and experiment with the "<u>Helps</u>" following each recipe. I also hope that you will always use your microwave oven creatively and to its fullest potential.

Thank you to my husband, LeRoy; daughters, Chan My and Larisa; and parents, Oliver and Mildred Garbe for their support, patience, and most of all, their confidence in me.

Thank you, also, to Arlene Hamernik, who made this booklet possible.

Joyce Bottcher

TABLE OF CONTENTS

NOTICE 7-8

APPETIZERS AND HORS D'OEUVRES:

    Bacon Wrapped Prunes 9
    Cheddar Cheese Soup 10
    Chinese Sweet and Sour Meatballs...11
    Double Cheese Quiche with
        Fresh Herbs.......................13
    Indonesian Beef Sate................15
    Mushroom Canapes....................17
    Stuffed Artichokes..................18
    Zesty Tomato Bouillion..............19

DESSERTS:

    Apple Slices with Spiced Cream 20
    Carmel Nut Torte 21-22
    Lemon Gingercake 23
    Mint Floating Island 24
    Mocha Layered Butter Cake.......25-26
    Pears in Almond Sauce 27
    Pots de Creme Vienna 28
    Rose Pears 29
    Sherbert Island Pie 30-31
    Swedish Apple Dessert...............32

MAIN DISHES:

    Beef and Mushroom Filled Crepes....33
    Round Steak Nicoise.............34-35

    Chicken Breasts Maltaise............36
    Chicken Breasts with Paprika Sauce.37
    Curried Chicken A L'Orange..........38

    Crab Spaghetti Ring.............39-40
    Fish with Oyster Stuffing.......41-42
    Golden Garlic Shrimp................43
    Quick Seafood Casserole.............44

MAIN DISHES (continued):

    Bourbon and Pecan Glazed Ham........45

    Italian Style Pork Chops............46
    Pork Chops in Sour Cream Sauce...47-48

MISCELLANEOUS:

    Fluffy Honey Dressing...............49
    Mushroom Seasoning..................50
    Old Fashioned Cole Slaw with Bacon..51
    Wild and White Rice Ring............52

SAUCES:

    Deluxe Mushroom Sauce...............53
    Italian Tomato Sauce................54
    Lemon Butter Dessert Sauce..........55
    Maltaise Sauce......................56
    Vanilla Sauce.......................57

VEGETABLES:

    Asparagus with Tomatoes and Cheese..58
    Escalloped Spinach Casserole........60
    Green Beans with Quick Mustard Sauce.61
    Italian Vegetable Medley.........62-63
    Parmesan Broccoli and Bacon.........64
    Stuffed Potatoes Supreme............65

About the Authors.......................66
Ordering Information....................67

NOTICE!

PLEASE READ BEFORE USING THESE RECIPES

The recipes in this book have been tested in counter top ovens of approximately 625 to 675 watts. If your oven is extremely higher or lower in wattage, cooking times will have to be altered.

REMEMBER - recipe timings are always used as a guide only because of the variables in microwave cooking, type of food being prepared and the voltage level (voltage can vary with each area, each home, as well as the time of day). Each individual oven is unique in its cooking and timing - simply get to know your oven and use it to the fullest.

All recipes have been microwaved on a high or full power setting unless a mid-way setting is stated.

A mid-way (50% power) has been used for some recipes where slower cooking will give a better product. This setting has been established because the variety of power settings available on many ovens are not consistent from one brand to another. For ovens with 2 settings only, use the lower power setting. The food will have to be checked for doneness during the last few minutes of cooking. Due to oven variations, the mid-way setting is even more of a 'guide only' than the timings for full power. To determine this mid-way (50% power) setting on ovens with several power levels, count the markings or words on the power control dial or panel - divide this number by 2 and set the power setting at this mid-way point.

For example, if your microwave oven has 10 power settings, divide the 10 by 2 and you'll find that the 5th setting down from the maximum power available will be the midway setting or approximately 50% power.

Food is to be covered during cooking only when stated in the recipe.

Ingredients were taken from normal storage places unless otherwise specified.

Large sized eggs were used.

Top quality ingredients should be used for best flavor and appearance. Butter, not a substitute, should be used for superior flavor.

Although it has been suggested that glass dishes be used for all these recipes, there are plastic-type containers designed for microwave cooking that can be substituted.

This is not intended to take the place of your manufacturer's cookbook but to supplement it.

Appetizers

BACON WRAPPED PRUNES

"Try these tempting tid-bits for your next party."

30 large pitted prunes
1/2 cup dark rum, bourbon or port wine
30 whole almonds or pecan halves
15 slices lean bacon

Combine prunes and 1/4 cup rum, bourbon or port in a 1 quart glass measure. Cover with plastic wrap. Microwave 2 minutes, shaking once to rearrange prunes in liquid.

Let stand, covered, until cool; add remaining 1/4 cup rum, bourbon or port. Cover and refrigerate 24 hours or up to two weeks.

Before serving, microwave bacon layered on paper towels for 6 to 7 minutes or until half cooked. Cut each slice in half.

Stuff prunes with almonds or pecans.

Wrap each prune with a half slice of bacon and secure with a toothpick.

Place 4 layers of paper towels on a glass or paper plate. Arrange 15 wrapped prunes in a circle on the plate. Microwave 2 minutes. Rotate plate and microwave 2 to 3 minutes or until bacon is crisp.

Makes 30 appetizers.

"Help" - To make ahead, wrap prunes in bacon and refrigerate. Add about 1 minute to the cooking time.

Try stuffed dates or watermelon pickles wrapped in bacon for a different taste.

CHEDDAR CHEESE SOUP

"This rich, hearty soup is ideal to serve on cold winter evenings."

2 tablespoons chopped onion
2 tablespoons chopped carrots
2 tablespoons chopped celery
2 tablespoons chopped parsley
2 tablespoons butter
3 cups rich chicken broth
1/4 teaspoon dry mustard
1/4 teaspoon paprika
1/8 teaspoon salt
2 tablespoons cornstarch
3 tablespoons light cream
1/4 pound(1 cup)grated sharp cheddar cheese
salt and white pepper

Combine onion, carrots, celery, parsley and butter in a 2-quart glass container. Microwave 2 minutes.

Add 1 cup chicken broth, dry mustard, paprika, and salt. Microwave 5 minutes.

Pour mixture into blender container and blend 30 to 60 seconds to liquify vegetables. Strain if desired.

Return mixture to 2-quart container. Stir cornstarch into cream and add to mixture, stirring constantly. Add remaining 2 cups chicken broth.

Microwave 7 minutes or until thickened and bubbling. Stir 2 times during last half of cooking period.

Add cheese, stirring well. Add salt and white pepper to taste. Garnish with croutons, popcorn, minced chives, chopped parsley or crumbled crisp bacon. Serves 4-6.

"Help" - Use a mid-way setting to reheat or the cheese may overcook and curdle.

CHINESE SWEET AND SOUR MEATBALLS

"Tiny meatballs, carrot rounds and green pepper slices in sweet-sour sauce make inviting hors d'oeuvres."

2 large carrots, sliced crosswise 1/8" thick
1 large green pepper, cut in 3/4" squares
1/2 pound ground lean pork
1/2 pound ground lean beef
1 cup soft bread crumbs
1/4 cup minced onion
1 large clove garlic, minced
2 tablespoons soy sauce
dash pepper
1 egg
1/2 cup chicken broth
1/4 cup red wine vinegar
1 teaspoon soy sauce
5 tablespoons brown sugar
1 tablespoon cornstarch
1/4 teaspoon paprika

Put carrots and green pepper in a 11x7 inch glass baking dish; set aside.

Combine ground pork, ground beef, bread crumbs, onion, garlic, soy sauce, pepper and egg. Mix lightly with a fork.

Make into 45 to 50 tiny meatballs; place on top of vegetables in dish.

Microwave 5 minutes. Turn and rearrange meatballs; microwave 2½ to 3½ minutes more or until meatballs are done. (Vegetables will be crunchy.) Set aside.

Combine remaining ingredients in a 4-cup glass measure. Microwave 1½ minutes; stir well and microwave 1 more minute.

Drain liquid from meatballs; add sauce and stir gently. Refrigerate several hours.

(continued)

CHINESE SWEET AND SOUR MEATBALLS (continued)

To serve, microwave 7 to 10 minutes or until heated through. Serve in a chafing dish with toothpicks.

Makes about 12 servings.

"Help" Be sure to make this a day in advance so flavors can blend well.

For Hawaiian Style Sweet and Sour Meatballs: microwave fresh pineapple chunks, covered, until hot; drain off juice and add to meatballs and sauce.

Try these as a delicious main dish. Make meatballs larger and serve on hot, fluffy, long-grain rice. Makes 4 to 5 servings.

To double recipe: double all ingredients but cook meatballs in 2 batches. Microwave double recipe of sauce together and combine with meatballs.

DOUBLE CHEESE QUICHE WITH FRESH HERBS

"This favorite luncheon dish is made 'new' with a Parmesan-flavored crust and a filling combining 2 kinds of cheese and fresh herbs."

3 eggs, beaten
1 ¼ cups light cream
1/4 teaspoon salt
1/8 teaspoon white pepper
2 tablespoons freshly grated Parmesan cheese
1 cup grated Swiss cheese
2 tablespoons minced fresh chives
2 tablespoons minced fresh parsley
1 ½ teaspoons minced fresh herbs, such as sweet marjoram, thyme or savory
1 baked 9-inch Parmesan Crust

Combine ingredients and pour into baked crust.

Microwave 6 minutes. Carefully stir cooked outside edges to center.

Microwave 4 minutes or until knife inserted near center comes out almost clean.

Let stand, covered with waxed paper, for 10 minutes. Serve warm or cold.

Makes 4 to 6 servings as a main dish or 8 to 12 servings as a first course.

PARMESAN CRUST

1/4 cup soft butter
2 tablespoons freshly grated parmesan cheese
1/2 cup flour
1/8 teaspoon salt
1 egg yolk

Cream butter and cheese together using a fork. Add flour and salt and mix until crumbly. Stir in egg yolk and mix very well. Dough should form a ball. (Mix with hands, if necessary.)
(continued)

DOUBLE CHEESE QUICHE WITH FRESH HERBS-con't

With fingers or fork, press into a 9-inch glass pie plate. Flute edges. (Crust will be quite thin.) Prick bottom and sides with fork.

Microwave 2 minutes; rotate dish. Microwave 1 to 1½ minutes more or until crust looks set. Makes one 9-inch crust.

"Help" - For a special first course, serve Tiny Quiches with Zesty Tomato Bouillion (page 15). Tiny Quiches take extra time to make, but can be made ahead and easily reheated in the microwave oven or served cold. (Quiche is never served hot, so there's no need to worry about overcooking when reheating.)

To make Tiny Quiches: Press about 1 tablespoon of Parmesan Crust into bottom and half way up sides of paper-lined microwave muffin cups or small custard cups. Microwave 6 for about 2½ minutes. Add about 1 tablespoon quiche filling. Microwave 6 for 45 to 60 seconds or until almost set. Let stand, covered with waxed paper 2 to 3 minutes. Carefully remove from pans and papers. Refrigerate. To heat - microwave 6 arranged in a circle on a paper plate or paper towel-lined glass plate, covered with plastic wrap, for 30 seconds. Let stand 1 minute and serve warm. Makes 14 to 18 individual quiches.

INDONESIAN BEEF SATE

"Tiny skewered beef strips, cooked on a lemon half and served with a spicy hot sauce, bring visions of an elaborate Indonesian rijsttafel."

3 tablespoons soy sauce
3 tablespoons lemon juice
1/4 cup minced onion
3 cloves garlic, minced
2 tablespoons dark brown sugar
3/4 teaspoon finely crushed coriander seeds
3/4 inch slice fresh gingerroot, cut in fourths
1/8 teaspoon freshly ground black pepper
2 to 2½ pounds steak, 3/4 inch thick
2 lemons
fresh coriander or parsley springs
Indonesian Peanut Sauce

Combine soy sauce, lemon juice, onion, garlic, brown sugar, coriander, gingerroot and pepper in 1½ quart bowl. Set aside.

Remove bone and excess fat from steak. Cut steak across grain in thin strips about 1/8 x 3/4 x 3 inches. For ease in cutting, meat should be slightly frozen.

Add meat to marinade, stirring to coat pieces. Marinate 4 to 5 hours, refrigerated. Stir ocassionally.

Cut lemons in half and place, cut sides down, on 2 glass plates or baking dishes (2 lemon halves per plate).

Thread 1 strip of meat on round toothpick, pushing meat towards 1 end. Put that end into lemon. Repeat with other meat strips until lemons are filled. Allow 12 to 14 strips per lemon half.

INDONESIAN BEEF SATÉ (continued)

Microwave 3 minutes. Rotate each lemon so meat will cook evenly. Microwave 2 to 3 minutes more for well-done meat, less for more rare meat.

With pancake turner, remove lemons to serving plate or drain off liquid from plate. Garnish with fresh coriander or parsley sprigs. Serve with Indonesian Peanut Sauce. About 15 servings or 50 hors d'ouvres.

INDONESIAN PEANUT SAUCE
1 cup grated sweetened coconut
1 cup water
1/2 cup salted Spanish peanuts (with skins on)
1/4 teaspoon ground ginger
1/4 teaspoon finely crushed coriander seeds
1/2 teaspoon ground cumin
4 large cloves garlic, minced
5 teaspoons lemon juice
1/4 teaspoon finely crushed red pepper

Make coconut milk by combining coconut and water in a 4-cup glass measure. Microwave 1½ to 2 minutes or until boiling: then boil 1 minute. Cool 10 minutes. Then place in blender container and blend about 1 minute until coconut is very finely chopped. Pour mixture through several layers of cheesecloth, squeezing out as much liquid as possible. There should be about 7/8 cup of liquid. Discard coconut.

Pulverize peanuts in blender. Combine peanuts, coconut milk and remaining ingredients in 4-cup glass measure. Microwave 4 minutes, stirring once. Refrigerate for 8 to 36 hours to blend flavors. To serve, Microwave 1 minute or until hot. Makes about 1½ cups.

"Help" - Taste sauce for seasoning after cooking. Sauce should be spicy "hot" and slightly tart. Add more red pepper if you want the "real" Indonesian Sauce.

MUSHROOM CANAPÉS

"Mushroom seasoning blends with cheese to make an unusual topping."

1/2 cup cool Mushroom Seasoning (page 50)
1/2 cup finely grated Swiss cheese
2 teaspoons grated Parmesan cheese
dash pepper
thin melba toast rounds
parsley to garnish

Combine Mushroom Seasoning, Swiss and Parmesan cheese and pepper; mix well. Spread on Melba rounds.

Arrange 8 to 10 rounds in a circle on a paper plate. Microwave 30 seconds or until the cheese melts.

Garnish each canapé with one parsley leaf. Serve immediately.

Makes 26 to 28 canapés.

"Help" - To soften refrigerated Mushroom Seasoning, microwave about 10 seconds.

Vary the flavor of these canapes by substituting finely grated cheddar cheese for the Swiss cheese.

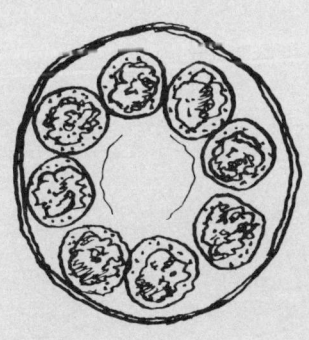

STUFFED ARTICHOKES

2 medium artichokes (3½" in diameter)
lemon juice
1/2 cup fine dry bread crumbs
1/4 cup Mushroom Seasoning (page 50)
1 tablespoon freshly grated Parmesan cheese
1/4 teaspoon salt
dash white pepper
2 tablespoons cream
2 teaspoons butter

Wash artichokes; cut off stem and prickly tips of leaves. Rub cut edges with lemon juice to prevent browning. Rinse well and wrap each artichoke tightly with plastic wrap.

Microwave 6 minutes or until bottom of artichoke is almost tender when pierced with a fork. Carefully remove plastic wrap and turn upside down to drain.

Spread leaves and remove fuzzy choke from the center, using a grapefruit spoon.

Combine bread crumbs, mushroom seasoning, Parmesan cheese, salt, pepper and cream; mix lightly with a fork. Put 1 teaspoon butter in center of each artichoke; then fill with stuffing. Set upright in an 8 x 4 inch glass loaf dish. Cover with plastic wrap and microwave 2 to 4 minutes or until hot. Cut in half or serve whole with melted butter. Makes 2 to 4 servings.

"Help" - Prepare artichokes ahead and cook about 5 minutes. Remove choke and refrigerate immediately. Right before serving, stuff and heat covered with plastic wrap for 4 to 6 minutes or until steaming hot.

Cooking time for 1 artichoke is about 4 minutes, 3 artichokes - 8 minutes; and for 4 artichokes about 10 minutes.

ZESTY TOMATO BOUILLON

"You'll like this served hot or icy cold for a low calorie snack or part of a light lunch."

4 whole cloves
1 slice onion
1 sprig parsley
1 small bay leaf
2 cups tomato juice
1 cup beef bouillon
dash to 1/8 teaspoon finely grated fresh lemon rind

Tie cloves, onion, parsley and bay leaf in a piece of cheese cloth or nylon net.

Combine all ingredients along with spice bag in a 2 quart glass container.

Microwave 10 minutes. Remove spice bag.

Serve hot with croutons or very cold with chopped cucumber and chives.

Makes 4 to 6 servings.

"Help" - If a spicier flavor is desired, add more flavorings or prepare ahead, leaving spice bag in until serving.

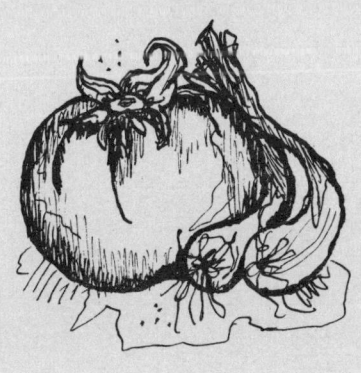

Desserts

APPLE SLICES WITH SPICED CREAM

"Few people believe that this simple recipe makes such a delicious dessert."

3 large cooking apples
3 tablespoons butter
2 tablespoons sugar
1/4 cup port wine
1/2 cup heavy cream
2 tablespoons sugar
1/8 teaspoon ground cinnamon

Pare, quarter and core apples; cut in 1/4 inch thick slices.

In a 1½ quart casserole, melt butter by microwaving for 30 seconds. Add apple slices; sprinkle with 2 tablespoons sugar and stir to coat apples.

Add wine; cover and microwave two minutes.

Stir. Cover and microwave 1½ to 2½ minutes. more or until apples are barely cooked. Do not over cook. Let stand covered 5 minutes.

Meanwhile, whip cream until stiff peaks form. Stir in sugar and cinnamon.

Serve warm apple slices in individual dessert dishes, topped with spiced cream.

Makes 4 servings.

"Help"- This dessert can be made ahead but it should be served warm. Reheat, covered, for 1 to 2 minutes or until just warm.

CARMEL NUT TORTE

"This traditional German torte - compact and flat rather than high and fluffy - is modernized with a creamy carmel topping."

6 egg yolks
1 cup sugar
1 teaspoon vanilla
3/4 teaspoon baking powder
1/2 cup finely chopped nuts
1 cup plus 2 tablespoons fine dry bread crumbs
6 egg whites (3/4 cup)
1/4 teaspoon cream of tartar
2 tablespoons sugar
1 cup heavy cream
5 teaspoons powdered sugar
10 chocolate covered carmels (about 3/4" squares)
2 tablespoons light cream
1 tablespoon butter

Have all ingredients at room temperature. See "Help" - page 23.

Beat egg yolks until thick and light-colored. Gradually beat in sugar. Stir in vanilla, baking powder and nuts; mix well. Thoroughly fold in crumbs.

Beat egg whites and cream of tartar until frothy. Gradually add sugar and beat until stiff peaks form.

Gently, but thoroughly, stir 1/3 of egg whites into crumb mixture; then fold in remaining egg whites.

Line 2 nine-inch round microwave-safe cake dishes with waxed paper. Pour batter into dishes.

CARMEL NUT TORTE - continued

Set one filled cake dish on an inverted glass saucer in microwave oven. Microwave 4 to 5 minutes on midway setting (or 4 minutes on high). Torte is done when it leaves edges of pan and center is done.

Set dish on wooden board and cool 5 minutes. Remove from dish, peel off waxed paper and cool completely on wire rack. Repeat with second layer.

When torte is cool, whip cream until stiff peaks form; stir in powdered sugar. Spread between layers and on sides and top. Refrigerate 15 to 30 minutes.

Meanwhile make carmel topping by combining carmels, cream and butter in a 1-cup glass measure. Microwave 1 minute; stir to melt carmels. Cool well until thickened.

Spread carmel topping on top of torte, letting it drizzle down sides if desired. Refrigerate about 30 minutes before serving.

Makes 10 - 14 servings.

"Help" - Room temperature egg whites beat to a higher volume than cold egg whites. Bring 2 to 4 large egg whites (1/4 to 1/2 cup) to room temperature by microwaving 10 to 15 seconds. Then stir immediately to distribute heat evenly and not cook any part of the egg white.

LEMON GINGERCAKE

"This will remind you of gingerbread, but with a light, new flavor."

2 tablespoons butter
1/2 cup brown sugar
1 egg
1/3 cup molasses
1/2 teaspoon grated lemon rind
1 cup flour
3/4 teaspoon soda
1/4 teaspoon ginger
1/4 teaspoon cinnamon
1/2 cup buttermilk

With electric mixer or by hand, cream butter and brown sugar until well blended. Add egg, mix well. Add molasses and grated lemon rind, mix well.

Sift together flour, soda, ginger and cinnamon; add alternately with buttermilk, stirring well after each addition.

Lightly butter a 6-cup microwave-safe ring mold or an 8-inch round glass dish with a glass set upright in center; sprinkle with sugar. Pour in batter.

Microwave 5 to 5½ minutes on high power, rotating dish 2 times. Let stand 5 minutes on flat surface. Invert onto serving dish.

Serve warm, sprinkled with powdered sugar; or split and fill with softened cream cheese and top with Lemon Butter Sauce (page 55). Makes 6 to 8 servings.

"Help" - For best results, ingredients should be at room temperature. Use your microwave oven carefully to help you - microwave liquid ingredients in a custard cup or glass measuring cup for a few seconds; then immediately stir to distribute the heat and not cook any part of the liquid. In this recipe, microwave the egg (removed from the shell) for 3 to 5 seconds and the buttermilk for 10 seconds being sure to stir each one immediately after microwaving.

MINT FLOATING ISLAND

"Eliminate the creme de menthe and chocolate to make a simple version of the French, 'Eggs in Snow'."

3 egg yolks, beaten
3 tablespoons sugar
dash salt
1 ½ cups milk
1 tablespoons green creme de menthe
1 egg white
dash salt
5 teaspoons sugar
1 ½ teaspoons chocolate syrup
chocolate syrup for garnish, if desired

Combine egg yolks, sugar, salt and milk in 1 quart glass measure; microwave 3 minutes. Stir very well. Microwave 1 to 1½ minutes more, stirring every 30 seconds. Cook until custard coats a metal spoon. Cool 15 minutes.

Stir in creme de menthe and pour into 4 glass dessert dishes. Set dishes on a glass tray or plate. Cool 15 minutes.

Beat egg white until frothy; add salt. Gradually add sugar and beat until soft peaks form (peaks fold over). Fold in chocolate syrup. Put a spoonful of meringue on top of each custard. Microwave custards on glass tray for 1½ to 2 minutes or until meringue is set.

Chill well. Drizzle with chocolate syrup before serving, if desired. Makes 4 servings.

"Help" - For 8 servings, double ingredients and microwave custard 7 minutes, then 1½ to 2 minutes more, stirring every 30 seconds. Cool. Cook meringues in 2 batches, 1½ to 2 minutes for each 4 servings.
For "Eggs in Snow", replace creme de menthe with 3/4 teaspoon vanilla and chocolate syrup with 1/4 teaspoon vanilla.

MOCHA LAYERED BUTTER CAKE

"Serve thin slices of this rich buttery cake layered with coffee-chocolate frosting."

2 cups sifted flour
1/2 teaspoon salt
1 ½ teaspoons baking powder
3/4 cup butter
1 ½ cups sugar
4 eggs (3/4 cup)
1 teaspoon vanilla
1/2 cup milk
Mocha Frosting.

Have all ingredients at room temperature (see "Help").

Sift together flour, salt and baking powder.

Cream butter until light. Add sugar gradually, beating constantly. Add eggs, one at a time, beating well after each. Add vanilla.

Alternately stir in (or use low speed of electric mixer) flour mixture and milk. Mix until well blended.

Line two 8 x 4 inch glass loaf pans with waxed paper; pour in batter.

Set cake on an inverted glass saucer in microwave oven. Microwave 1 cake at a time for 5 to 7 minutes on mid-way setting or until cake is done.

Set pan on wooden board and cool for 5 minutes. Remove from pan, peel off waxed paper and cool completely. Repeat with second layer.

Divide 1 cake into 3 layers using toothpicks as guides. Spread Mocha Frosting between layers. Frost sides and top, swirling frosting. Makes 12 to 14 servings. (continued)

MOCHA LAYERED BUTTER CAKE   continued

MOCHA FROSTING

3/4 cup butter
1/2 ounce (½ square) semi-sweet chocolate
1 tablespoon instant coffee granules
1/2 teaspoon hot water
1 ½ cups powdered sugar

In a medium size glass bowl, microwave butter and chocolate for 1 to 1¼ minutes; stir well to melt chocolate. Cool completely but do not chill.

Dissolve cofee granules in hot water. Stir dissolved coffee into cool butter mixture; add powdered sugar and beat with electric mixer until stiff peaks form. Frost cake.

"Help" - Use the following time guides to bring refrigerated ingredients to room temperature: 3/4 cup butter--5 seconds, 4 eggs (removed from shell)--15 seconds, 1/2 cup milk--10 seconds. Be sure to stir immediately after microwaving to distribute heat evenly and not have some cooked areas. (see "Help" - page 19).

As frosting cools, it will become very firm. You may use a pastry tube to further decorate cake. If frosting becomes too firm, microwave for only a few seconds and stir well to soften.

For a very high cake, split second cake into layers and add 1 or 2 layers to first cake, spreading frosting very sparingly between layers.

Serve second cake, sliced and topped with Lemon Butter Dessert Sauce (page 55)

The frosted cake freezes very well.

PEARS IN ALMOND SAUCE

"These pears cooked in an almond-flavored pudding are delicious served for special occasions or everyday meals."

1/3 cup butter
1/2 cup sugar
5 teaspoons flour
1/2 cup milk
1/2 cup sliced almonds
4 large ripe pears, peeled, halved & cored.

Combine butter, sugar, flour, milk and almonds in 4-cup glass measure. Microwave 2 minutes.

Stir well and microwave 1 to 1½ minutes or until bubbling.

Place pears, tops toward center and cut side down, in a 10 inch glass pie plate. Set a glass or custard cup, open end up, in center of plate.

Pour pudding mixture over pears. Microwave 5 to 6 minutes, rotating dish two times. Cook until pears are just tender. Serve warm or cold.

Makes 4 to 8 servings.

"Help" - Try this with peeled, halved and cored fresh peaches or apples.

POTS de CREME VIENNA

"Serve very small portions of this rich chocolate-flavored dessert."

1½ cups strong coffee
1 pkg. (12 oz.) semi-sweet chocolate chips
2 eggs
2 tablespoons sugar
pinch salt
1 teaspoon vanilla
1/2 teaspoon ground cinnamon
1/2 cup heavy cream
2 tablespoons sugar
1/8 teaspoon cinnamon

Combine ½ cup coffee and chocolate chips in a small glass bowl. Microwave about 1 minute; stir well to melt chocolate.

Put eggs, 2 tablespoons sugar, salt, vanilla, cinnamon and chocolate mixture in blender container. Blend 5 seconds. Stop blender and scrape sides with rubber spatula. Remove center cover from blender.

Bring remainder of the coffee (1 cup) just to boiling by microwaving about 2 minutes.

Immediately turn on blender and pour boiling coffee slowly through center opening. Stop blender and scrape sides. Blend about 45 seconds more.

Pour into 8 pots de creme cups or small dessert dishes. Chill at least 2 hours.

Before serving, whip cream and add sugar and cinnamon. Top each serving with 1 tablespoonful of whipped cream.

Makes 8 servings.

"Help"- Be sure to use 'real' chocolate chips-flavored chocolate doesn't melt well.

You may substitute 1½ to 2 tablespoons instant coffee and 1½ cups water for strong coffee.

ROSE' PEARS

"Serve as a refreshing beginning or ending to a special brunch or luncheon."

4 firm, ripe, medium-size Bartlett pears
1 cup Rose' wine
1/2 cup sugar
1/2 inch fresh gingerroot, quartered
1 cinnamon stick, broken in 4 pieces

Peel, halve and core pears. Place pears in a 1½-quart casserole.

In a 2 cup glass measure, combine wine, sugar and spices. Microwave 2 to 3 minutes or until almost boiling.

Pour hot wine mixture along with pieces of gingerroot and cinnamon over pear halves in casserole. Cover with plastic wrap.

Microwave 1 minute, rotate dish if necessary, and microwave 1 minute more or until pears are barely soft to the touch.

Let stand, covered, until cool. Remove spices; place pears, cut side down, in 4 dessert dishes. Pour wine mixture over pears. Refrigerate. Serve cold.

Makes 4 servings.

"Help" - For a spicier flavor, leave spices in dishes while chilling.

Cooking time will vary according to size and temperature of pears. D'Anjou or Comice pears may be used, but may need a little more cooking time.

Do not use ground spices--they darken the liquid and fall to the bottom of dessert dishes.

SHERBET ISLAND PIE

"Enjoy this light frozen pie on a balmy summer day."

1/4 cup butter
2 cups grated or flaked coconut
2 teaspoons unflavored gelatin
2 tablespoons cold water
1 tablespoon cornstarch
1/4 cup sugar
dash salt
1 cup milk
1/4 teaspoon lemon juice
1/2 teaspoon vanilla
1 pint sherbet, any flavor
1/3 cup heavy cream
2 egg whites
1/8 teaspoon cream of tartar
1/4 cup sugar

In a 9-inch glass pie plate, microwave butter for 30 seconds. Stir in coconut. Press mixture on bottom and sides of pie plate. Microwave about 2 minutes. If sides fall down, gently push them back in place with a fork. Cool.

Combine gelatin with cold water; set aside.

In 2-cup glass measuring cup, combine cornstarch, sugar, salt, milk and lemon juice. Microwave 3 minutes.

Stir well; then microwave 30 to 60 seconds or until boiling. Stir in gelatin and vanilla. Cool until thickened.

With melon ball cutter or teaspoon measuring spoon, make small sherbet balls; place on cooky sheet and keep frozen.

(continued)

SHERBET ISLAND PIE (continued)

Beat egg whites and cream of tartar until frothy. Gradually add sugar, beating until stiff peaks form; set aside.

With same beater, beat cream until stiff peaks form.

Fold whipped cream into thickened gelatin mixture; then fold in beaten egg whites.

Pour gelatin mixture about 1/4 inch deep on bottom of coconut crust. Top with sherbet balls. Then pour remaining gelatin mixture around sherbet balls, filling in between balls, but leaving some sherbet showing through. Freeze until solid.

Before serving, remove from freezer for about 15 minutes.

Makes 6 to 8 servings.

"Help" - For a change, try a toasted coconut crust. Spread coconut in glass pie plate. Microwave 6 to 7 minutes or until coconut is golden. Stir several times and watch carefully so coconut doesn't burn. Then combine with butter and proceed with crust.

SWEDISH APPLE DESSERT

"This Swedish 'cake' is best served warm, topped generously with cold Vanilla Sauce."

1/2 cup butter
2 3/4 cups fine dry bread crumbs
3 tablespoons sugar
1½ teaspoons cinnamon
2¼ cups freshly-made applesauce, sweetened to taste
cold Vanilla Sauce (page 57).

Melt butter in an 11 x 7 inch glass baking dish by microwaving 45 to 60 seconds.

Mix crumbs, sugar and cinnamon and add to butter; stir well.

Microwave 6 minutes or until crumbs are golden brown. Stir well 2 or 3 times during cooking.

Butter a 1 or 1½ quart glass casserole. Make layers of crumbs and applesauce, starting and ending with crumbs.

Microwave 9 minutes.

Serve warm with cold Vanilla Sauce.

Makes 6 to 8 servings.

"Help" - This is easily made ahead and reheated. Four servings in individual dishes take 1½ to 2 minutes to heat.

If applesauce is cold, increase cooking time to 11 minutes.

Main Dishes

BEEF AND MUSHROOM FILLED CREPES

"These crepes, with a rich creamy filling, are made quickly and economically with ground beef."

2 cups sliced fresh mushrooms
1 medium onion, chopped
1 clove garlic, minced
1 pound lean ground beef
2 tablespoons flour
1 teaspoon salt
1/4 teaspoon pepper
dash Worchestershire sauce
1 can (10 3/4 oz.) cream of mushroom soup
1/2 cup dairy sour cream
1/4 cup chopped pimento
10 to 14 cooked crepes
1/4 cup sharp old English process cheese spread

Combine mushrooms, onion, and garlic in a 1½ to 2 quart glass casserole. Crumble ground beef on top. Microwave 5 minutes, stirring once.

Stir in flour, salt, pepper, Worchestershire sauce and soup. Microwave 3½ to 4½ minutes or until bubbling. Stir in sour cream and pimento.

Fill crepes generously with meat mixture; roll up and place close together in 11 x 7 inch glass baking dish. It may be necessary to place a few crepes in another dish or on serving plate to heat.

(continued)

BEEF AND MUSHROOM FILLED CREPES (continued)

Soften cheese by microwaving 15 to 30 seconds; spoon over center of each rolled crepe. Cover with waxed paper. Microwave 2 minutes or until crepes are heated, rotating dish once. Makes 10 to 14 filled crepes.

"Help" - Filled crepes may be prepared ahead and refrigerated until serving time. Heat, covered, on a mid-way setting for 4 to 5 minutes, rotating dish once.

ROUND STEAK NICOISE

"Typical seasonings of Nice, France, enhance round steak to make it very special."

1 medium onion
1 large clove garlic, minced
3 tablespoons olive or salad oil
1/3 cup fine dry bread crumbs
2 teaspoons minced fresh basil (or 1/2
   teaspoon dried and crumbled basil)
1/4 teaspoon salt
1/4 teaspoon paprika
1/4 teaspoon freshly grated black pepper
1 pound top or tip round steak, ½-inch thick
3 tablespoons flour
1 egg, beaten
3 medium tomatoes
salt and freshly ground black pepper
16 medium pitted ripe olives
1 teaspoon minced fresh basil (or 1/4 teaspoon
   dried, crumbled basil)
8 anchovy fillets, if desired

Peel onion; cut in half lengthwise and slice thinly to make long thin slivers.

Combine onion, garlic and oil in 11 x 7 inch glass baking dish. Stir to coat onion with oil and arrange evenly in dish. (continued)

ROUND STEAK NICOISE (continued)

Combine bread crumbs, basil, salt, paprika and pepper; set aside.

Cut steak into 3 or 4 pieces. Pound in flour on both sides.

Dip one side in egg, then in crumb mixture; lay crumb-side up on top of onions in pan. Repeat with other pieces.

Cover with plastic wrap. Microwave 6 1/2 minutes, rotating dish once.

While steak is cooking, peel tomatoes, quarter and cut each quarter in half (for 8 wedges per tomato). Place in colander and let stand to drain.

Carefully remove plastic wrap. Turn and rearrange steak. Spoon a small amount of egg on top and sprinkle with remaining crumbs.

Microwave, uncovered, 3 to 3½ minutes.

Remove to warm serving plate. Sprinkle with salt and pepper. Cover tightly with foil and let stand 5 minutes.

Microwave pan drippings 30 seconds. Add tomato wedges, ripe olives and basil. Microwave 1 minute.

Stir and microwave 1 more minute or until very hot. Spoon vegetables and some juices around meat. Top with anchovy fillets, if desired. Makes 3 to 4 servings.

"Help" - For very juicy and tender round steak, be sure to use a top quality top or tip round steak. Do not overcook. Check for doneness after standing time.

CHICKEN BREASTS MALTAISE

"A superb dish--moist, tender chicken breasts served on rice--topped with rich, buttery Maltaise Sauce."

3 large chicken breasts (about 3 pounds)
3 tablespoons butter
2 tablespoons freshly squeezed orange juice
1/4 teaspoon paprika
3 to 4 cups hot cooked long-grain rice
3/4 cup Maltaise Sauce (page 56)

Skin, bone and cut chicken breasts in half. Place in 6 x 10 inch glass baking dish.

In custard cup, microwave butter for 30 seconds. Stir in orange juice and paprika.

Brush tops of chicken generously with butter mixture. Cover with waxed paper. Microwave 5 minutes.

Turn chicken breasts over; rearrange if necessary. Brush with remaining butter mixture. Cover with waxed paper. Microwave 1 to 2 minutes or until just about done. Let stand, covered, for 5 minutes.

Place rice on large serving platter; arrange chicken on rice and pour pan drippings on top. Top each chicken breast with warm Maltaise Sauce. Serve immediately.

Makes 3 to 6 servings.

"Help" - Maltaise Sauce can be made ahead and reheated carefully on mid-way setting. Heat about 10 seconds, stir and repeat until just warm.

CHICKEN BREASTS WITH PAPRIKA SAUCE

"An unusual combination of seasoning blends together to make this deliciously flavored chicken dish."

3 tablespoons butter
1 ¼ teaspoons paprika
1 teaspoon lemon juice
8 large mushroom caps, sliced
3 large chicken breasts, halved (about 3 lbs.)
1/4 cup slivered almonds
6 tablespoons straight sherry
3/4 teaspoon worchestershire sauce
salt and freshly ground black pepper
5 ½ teaspoon flour
1 tablespoon chicken broth
1/3 cup dairy sour cream

Microwave butter for 30 seconds in 11 x 7 inch glass baking dish. Stir in paprika and lemon juice; spread evenly in pan.

Place mushroom slices on top of butter. Arrange chicken, skin side down on mushrooms. Cover with waxed paper and microwave 8 minutes, rotating dish once.

Turn chicken pieces (mushrooms will be on top of chicken now). Top with slivered almonds.

Combine sherry and Worcestershire sauce; pour around chicken. Microwave 7 to 9½ minutes, uncovered. Remove to serving platter, season to taste with salt and pepper and cover tightly with foil. Let stand 10 minutes.

Combine flour and broth; add to pan drippings. Microwave 1½ minutes or until bubbling. Stir in sour cream and microwave 30 seconds to heat. Do not boil. Serve sauce over chicken or separately. Makes 3 to 6 servings.

"Help" - Chicken breasts may be skinned and boned. Allow slightly less cooking time.

CURRIED CHICKEN A'L'ORANGE

"Golden brown chicken, mild curry, orange sauce and fresh orange rounds make this dish delightful to look at and to taste."

1 broiler-fryer (2½ to 3 pounds), cut up
1/2 cup orange juice
2 teaspoons curry powder
1/2 teaspoon paprika
1/8 teaspoon tumeric
1/3 cup orange marmalade
2 tablespoons prepared mustard
1 large orange
salt
4 teaspoons cornstarch
2 tablespoons cold water

Arrange chicken, skin-side down in a 11 x 7 inch glass baking dish, placing meatier part of pieces to outside.

Combine orange juice, curry powder, paprika, tumeric, orange marmalade and mustard in a 2-cup glass measure. Microwave 2 minutes; stir and pour over chicken.

Microwave 7 minutes. Turn chicken and baste each piece thoroughly with sauce. Microwave 12 to 14 minutes or until chicken is done.

While chicken is cooking, cut orange into 1/2 inch thick rounds, leaving peeling on. Cut each round in half. Reserve for garnishing.

Remove chicken to a serving platter; sprinkle with salt and garnish with orange rounds. Cover and let stand while finishing sauce.

In 2-cup glass measure, combine cornstarch and water. Add pan juices. Microwave about 30 seconds; stir well and microwave 30 to 60 seconds more until bubbly and thick. Add salt to taste. Serve sauce separately or pour over chicken. Serve with hot, cooked rice.

Makes 4 to 5 servings.

"Help" - If you like a milder curry flavor, reduce curry powder to one teaspoon.

CRAB SPAGHETTI RING

"Try this elegant-looking, ring-shaped casserole filled with green peas and topped with rich mushroom sauce."

1 ½ cups uncooked Italian spaghetti, broken into 1 to 2" pieces (3 cups cooked)
6 tablespoons minced green pepper
2 tablespoons butter
4 eggs, beaten
2 cups milk
1 ½ cups soft bread crumbs (about 2½ slices)
1 ½ cups grated cheddar cheese
3 tablespoons chopped pimento
1 can (6½ oz.) crabmeat, undrained
1/2 teaspoon salt
1/4 teaspoon white pepper
1 tablespoon butter
2 tablespoons fine dry bread crumbs
1 to 2 cups fresh or frozen peas, cooked and drained
Deluxe Mushroom Sauce (page 53)

Cook spaghetti in microwave or conventionally until just tender; drain and reserve.

Place green pepper in 2 quart glass casserole; top with butter and microwave 1½ minutes.

Add eggs, milk, bread crumbs, cheese, pimento, undrained crabmeat, salt, white pepper and cooked spaghetti; stir well.

Pour into 6-cup microwave-safe ring mold (mold will be very full). Cover with wax paper. Microwave 8 minutes, rotating dish once.

Stir outside cooked edges to center. Microwave, covered with wax paper, 6 to 8 minutes more or until knife inserted near center comes out just about clean. Let stand, covered, 5 to 10 minutes.

(continued)

CRAB SPAGHETTI RING (continued)

Meanwhile, melt 1 tablespoon butter by microwaving 15 seconds; add dry bread crumbs and microwave 1 to 1½ minutes or until golden brown. Stir once or twice.

Invert mold onto a large serving plate and sprinkle with crumb mixture. Fill center with hot, cooked peas. Serve with Deluxe Mushroom Sauce.

Makes 6 to 8 servings.

"Help" - One cup diced, cooked ham or chicken or 1 can (6½ ounces) tuna (flaked and drained) may be substituted for the crabmeat.

If you don't want to unmold this, microwave it right in the 2-quart casserole in which it was mixed. You may need to stir one time during the second cooking period. This can be microwaved on a mid-way setting for 13 to 15 minutes. Using the mid-way setting, it would not be necessary to stir.

FISH WITH OYSTER STUFFING

"Economical large fish fillets are turned into a special dish when filled with oyster stuffing."

2 tablespoons butter
1/2 teaspoon paprika
1/4 cup butter
1/3 cup minced celery and celery leaves
1 tablespoon minced onion
1 tablespoon minced parsley
1/4 teaspoon salt
dash white pepper
1/3 cup chopped cooked oysters
2 cups soft white and rye bread crumbs
1 tablespoon dry white wine
2 large fish fillets 3/4 to 1 inch thick
  (about 3/4 pound each)
salt and white pepper
minced chives

In a 11 x 7 inch glass baking dish, melt two tablespoons butter by microwaving 30 seconds. Stir in paprika. Coat dish with butter; pour out remaining butter and reserve.

In a 1-quart casserole or measuring cup, combine 1/4 cup butter, celery, onion, parsley. Microwave for 1 minute. Add 1/4 teaspoon salt, dash white pepper, oysters, bread crumbs and wine. Toss gently.

Place fillets in butter-coated dish. Using a sharp knife, cut each fillet lengthwise almost through to the other side, forming a pocket. Sprinkle inside of each pocket with salt and pepper. Fill with stuffing and fold top of each fillet over stuffing. Secure with toothpicks. Drizzle with remaining butter and paprika mixture.

(continued)

FISH WITH OYSTER STUFFING (continued)

Microwave, covered with waxed paper, for 5 to 6 minutes until top middle of fish flakes with a fork. Let stand, covered, on wooden board for 5 minutes. Check center bottom of largest fillet for doneness.

Season with salt and pepper. Sprinkle top with minced chives. Serve from baking dish or remove to a hot platter. Pour pan juices over top, if desired.

Makes 5 to 6 servings.

"Help" - Any non-oily fish such as pollock, haddock or pike works well in this recipe. Try using a whole fish instead of fillets.

All white bread crumbs may be used, however, part rye crumbs add interest. Do not be tempted to use a dark rye bread such as pumpernickel.

GOLDEN GARLIC SHRIMP

"Cooks-in-a-hurry will enjoy preparing this tasty dish."

1 pound ready-to-cook frozen shrimp
2 tablespoons butter
1/3 cup dry bread crumbs
2 tablespoons medium or dry sherry
1 clove garlic pressed
dash cayenne
dash white pepper
2 tablespoons butter
1/2 to 3/4 cup fine soft bread crumbs
   (1 slice bread)
salt
lemon wedges, if desired

Thaw shrimp in package or on pie plate for 3½ to 4 minutes on midway setting, rearranging shrimp once during thawing time. Let stand, covered, for 5 minutes. Shrimp should still be cold.

Melt butter in glass measuring cup by microwaving for 30 seconds; add dry bread crumbs; stir well. Microwave 1½ to 2 minutes or until crumbs are golden brown; stirring once. Stir well and set aside.

Drain shrimp and pat dry with paper towels. Put in shallow serving dish or casserole.

Combine sherry, pressed garlic juice and cayenne; pour over shrimp. Top with soft bread crumbs and dot with remaining butter. Microwave 2 minutes; stir well and microwave 2 to 2½ minutes more.

Sprinkle with salt. Let stand five minutes, covered. Top with golden bread crumbs. Garnish with lemon wedges, if desired. Makes 4 to 5 servings.

"Help" - Try the golden bread crumb topping with other dishes that call for au gratin (crumbs and butter topping that is usually placed under the broiler to brown).

QUICK SEAFOOD CASSEROLE

"Keep most ingredients for this on your cupboard shelf for the times you need a last-minute, but special, main dish."

2 to 3 tablespoons minced scallions, including green tops
1 cup chopped celery
2 cans (10 3/4 ounces each) cream of mushroom soup
1 to 2 cans (4½ ounces each) tiny shrimp, drained
1 can (6½ ounces) crabmeat, drained & flaked
1/2 cup whole cashews
1 can (3 ounces) or 2 cups chow mein noodles
whole cashews

Combine scallions and celery in a 1½ quart casserole and microwave, covered, for 3 minutes.

Add soup, shrimp, crabmeat, cashews and 1½ cups cups chow mein noodles; stir carefully.

Microwave 5 to 6 minutes or until hot, stirring carefully once.

Slightly crumble remaining chow mein noodles and sprinkle on top. Garnish with whole cashews.

Makes 4 to 5 servings.

"Help" - To stretch this recipe without loss of flavor, another cup of chow mein noodles may be added.

BOURBON AND PECAN GLAZED HAM

"Picture this pecan-studded ham as the main attraction of a festive buffet-style dinner."

1 pre-cooked or ready-to-eat ham (2½-3 lbs.)
2 tablespoons bourbon
1/4 cup brown sugar
2 tablespoons bourbon
1/8 teaspoon ground cloves, if desired
1/4 to 1/2 cup pecan halves

Place ham, fat side down in 8 x 8 inch glass baking dish. Pour 2 tablespoons bourbon over ham.

Microwave 12 minutes, covered with waxed paper.

Turn ham fat side up. Combine brown sugar, 2 tablespoons bourbon, cloves (if used) and pecans; spoon over ham.

Microwave 5 to 7 minutes more or until meat thermometer registers 125 degrees Fahrenheit. Let stand, covered with foil, 20 minutes to complete cooking. (Temperature will rise to 140 degrees during standing time.)

Makes 6 to 10 servings.

"Help" - For ready-to-eat hams over 3½ pounds, microwave 12 minutes per pound on midway setting (50% power). Turn ham over when about 2/3 cooking time is finished. Add glaze during the last 1/3 of the cooking time.

ITALIAN-STYLE PORK CHOPS

"Try these as a quick main dish, served with hot buttered noodles and Parmesan cheese."

1 cup Italian Tomato Sauce (page 54)
4 pork chops, 1 inch thick (about 2 lbs.)
salt
freshly ground pepper
1/4 to 1/2 cup shredded mozarella cheese

Pour 1/3 cup Italian Tomato Sauce in 11 x 7 inch glass baking dish. Place pork chops on top, putting meatiest parts to outside. Top with 1/3 cup more sauce.

Cover with waxed paper; microwave 5 minutes.

Turn and rearrange chops. Spoon remaining 1/3 cup sauce over chops. Cover with waxed paper and microwave 10 to 12 minutes more.

Sprinkle with salt and pepper. Top each chop with shredded cheese. Let stand, covered for 5 to 10 minutes.

Makes 4 servings.

"Help" - Be sure not to overcook pork chops. Check for doneness after standing time.

Try this recipe with veal chops.

PORK CHOPS WITH SOUR CREAM SAUCE

"These pork chops are juicy and tender inside a crumb breading."

4 pork chops, 1-inch thick (about 2 lbs.)
1/2 cup fine dry bread crumbs
1/4 teaspoon dried thyme, crushed
1/2 teaspoon paprika
1/2 teaspoon salt
1/4 teaspoon pepper
1 to 2 tablespoons flour
1 egg, slightly beaten
1/2 cup strong chicken broth
3 tablespoons sweet vermouth
1/3 cup dairy sour cream

Trim fat from edges of pork chops, leaving 1/8 inch of fat.

Combine crumbs, thyme, paprika, salt and pepper.

Sprinkle flour on one side of pork chops. Dip same side in egg, then into crumb mixture.

Place crumb-side up in 10 inch glass pie plate or 11 x 7 inch glass dish. Microwave 5 min..

Pour broth and vermouth around chops. Cover with plastic wrap; microwave 7 minutes.

Carefully remove plastic wrap. Turn and rearrange chops. Top with a little egg and sprinkle with remaining crumb mixture.

Cover with new plastic wrap. Microwave 6 to 7 minutes more.

Put chops on serving plate, cover and let stand 5 to 10 minutes.

(continued)

PORK CHOPS WITH SOUR CREAM SAUCE (continued)

To make sauce, microwave pan drippings for 30 seconds in a 1 cup glass measure. (Strain if desired.) Stir in sour cream and microwave 30 seconds or until hot. Do not boil.

Serve sauce in separate bowl to spoon over chops.

Makes 4 servings.

"Help" - Pork chops are excellent cooked in the microwave oven - the secret is to use thick pork chops (one inch are best) and not to overcook them. If you must use thin chops (1/2 inch thin) for this recipe, microwave 5 minutes, then 4 minutes, then 3 minutes and let stand about 5 minutes.

Miscellaneous

FLUFFY HONEY DRESSING

"This dressing goes well with all fresh fruits and will even please most non-honey lovers."

2 eggs, well beaten
2 tablespoons lime juice
1/2 cup honey
dash salt
1 tablespoon butter
1 cup heavy cream, whipped

In 2-cup glass measure, combine eggs, lime juice, honey and salt. Beat well with wire whisk.

Microwave 2 minutes. Whisk well.

Microwave 45 to 60 seconds or until just boiling and thickened. Do not overcook. Whisk well; then add butter.

Refrigerate until thoroughly cooled. Fold into whipped cream. Chill well.

Serve with fresh fruit for a salad or dessert. Keeps 2 to 3 days in refrigerator.

Makes 1 1/2 cups.

"Help" - This recipe can be halved; but be very careful not to overcook.

MUSHROOM SEASONING

"What a wonderful way to use up fresh mushroom stems or to conveniently preserve mushrooms for later use!"

1/2 pound fresh mushroom stems and pieces
2 to 4 tablespoons shallots or onions, minced
1/4 cup butter
1/4 to 1/2 teaspoon salt
dash white pepper

Chop mushrooms very finely. There should be about 2 cups.

Put mushrooms in a clean towel, small jelly bag or several layers of cheesecloth and squeeze out as much juice as possible. (Save juice for seasoning soups, sauces or stews.)

In small glass casserole, sauté shallots in butter by microwaving 1 minute.

Add mushrooms and microwave 2 to 3 minutes or until most juice has evaporated.

Stir in seasonings.

Store in covered glass jar in refrigerator for up to 2 weeks or in freezer for up to 2 months. Makes about 1 cup.

"Help" - Duxelles, (the classic name for this delicious seasoning) are used wherever a mushroom flavor is wanted. Use in sauces, gravies, stuffings, scrambled eggs, hors d'oeuvres, and crepe fillings.

OLD FASHIONED COLE SLAW WITH BACON

"Try the dressing with cold sliced potatoes, sliced hard-cooked eggs and fresh minced chives for a luscious potato salad."

1/2 to 3/4 cup Old Fashioned Dressing
2 cups finely shredded green cabbage
2 cups finely shredded red cabbage
6 slices bacon, cooked and crumbled

Before serving, toss dressing with cabbage. Sprinkle with bacon. Makes 6 to 8 servings.

OLD FASHIONED DRESSING

4 egg yolks, beaten
2 tablespoons cold water
3 tablespoons white wine vinegar
3/4 teaspoon dry mustard
1 tablespoon sugar
3/4 teaspoon salt
dash white pepper
1 cup dairy sour cream

Combine egg yolks, water, vinegar, dry mustard, sugar, salt and pepper in a 2-cup glass measure. Beat well with wire whisk.

Microwave 30 seconds; stir very well.

Microwave 15 to 30 seconds more or until thickened. Do not overcook. (Mixture may look slightly curdled, but this will disappear when added to sour cream.)

Cool well. Whisk in dairy sour cream. Keeps in refrigerator for about 3 to 4 days.

Makes 1 3/4 cups.

"Help" - If dressing is too spicy for your taste, reduce dry mustard to 1/2 teaspoon.

WILD AND WHITE RICE RING

"A combination rice dish elegantly served in a ring-mold shape."

1 ¼ cups water
1/2 cup wild rice
1 ¼ cups rich chicken broth
1 cup long-grained white rice
1 ¼ teaspoons salt
1/4 cup butter, cut in small pieces
3/4 cup minced onions
1 cup minced celery
1/4 teaspoon white pepper
1/4 cup minced parsley

In 2 quart casserole, microwave water and wild rice, covered, for 4 to 5 minutes or until boiling. Let stand, covered, for ten minutes.

Add chicken broth, white rice, and salt. Microwave, covered, for 6 minutes or until boiling. Let stand, covered, for 10 minutes.

Add butter, onions, celery, white pepper and parsley. Microwave 10 to 12 minutes or until liquid is absorbed and rice is almost tender. Let stand, covered, for 10 minutes to finish cooking.

Press rice firmly into a 5 to 6 cup ring mold. Let stand 5 minutes. Carefully run a knife blade around edges and center of mold. Invert on serving plate.

Makes 6 to 8 servings.

"Help" - To make ahead, invert onto the serving plate, cover with plastic wrap and refrigerate. To serve - microwave, covered with plastic wrap, for 3 to 4 minutes or until steaming hot. Be sure to use a serving plate that doesn't have metal trim.

Sauces

DELUXE MUSHROOM SAUCE

"Try this creamy full-flavored sauce over any food that can be enhanced by a rich mushroom sauce."

2 tablespoons butter
2 cups sliced fresh mushrooms
1/4 cup butter
1 small clove garlic, pressed*
1 small shallot, pressed*
1/4 cup flour
1/4 teaspoon salt
1/8 teaspoon white pepper
1 cup beef broth
2/3 cup heavy or light cream

In a 1 quart glass dish, microwave 2 tablespoons butter for 30 seconds or until melted. Add mushrooms, stir and microwave 2½ minutes. Set aside.

In a 4-cup glass measure, microwave ¼ cup butter, pressed garlic and shallot juices for 30 seconds or until butter is melted.

Stir in flour, salt and pepper. Microwave 45 seconds. Beat well with wooden spoon or wire whisk.

Slowly add beef broth, beating constantly.

Microwave 2½ to 3 minutes or until thick and bubbly, stirring 2 times after about 1½ minutes of cooking time.

Slowly add cream, beating well. Stir in mushrooms and accumulated juice.

Microwave about 45 seconds or until hot. May be made ahead and reheated. Makes about 2 cups.

(continued)

DELUXE MUSHROOM SAUCE (continued)

"Help" - *There are 3 ways to get the desired subtle garlic and shallot flavor for this sauce: 1. use a garlic press as indicated in the ingredient list; 2. spear crushed garlic and shallot on toothpicks, cook with sauce and remove before serving; 3. use 1/4 teaspoon minced shallot and 1/8 teaspoon minced garlic, cook with sauce and sieve through fine sieve before adding cream.

ITALIAN TOMATO SAUCE

"Serve this flavorful sauce on pasta or meats to add an Italian touch."

1/3 to 1/2 cup chopped onion
1 clove garlic, minced
1 medium carrot, minced
2 to 4 sprigs parsley, minced
1 cup sliced mushrooms, if desired
2 tablespoons butter
2 tablespoons oil
1 can (15 ounces) tomato puree
1 cup beef broth
1 cup dry red wine
1/2 teaspoon salt
1/4 teaspoon pepper
1/4 teaspoon dried crushed rosemary
1/4 teaspoon dried oregano
1/2 teaspoon dried basil

In a deep 2-quart glass container, combine onion, garlic, carrot, parsley, mushrooms, butter and oil. Microwave 3 minutes.

Add remaining ingredients. Microwave about 25 minutes or until thickened, stirring occasionally. Makes about 4½ cups sauce.

"Help" - For a spicier flavor, refrigerate several hours or overnight and reheat. For meat sauce, add ½ to 1 pound lean ground beef to vegetables and microwave 5 minutes to cook meat; OR add cooked meatballs and juices toward end of cooking time. Either way, use ¼ cup less beef broth.

LEMON BUTTER DESSERT SAUCE

"Try this buttery refreshing lemon sauce over simple cakes, fruit or vanilla ice cream."

1/3 cup water
1 egg
2/3 cup sugar
1/2 teaspoon grated lemon rind
1/4 cup butter, cut into pieces
2 tablespoons lemon juice

In 2-cup glass measure, measure water; add egg and beat well with wire whisk.

Stir in sugar, lemon rind and butter

Microwave 2 minutes; whisk well.

Microwave 45 to 60 seconds or until just about boiling and <u>slightly</u> thickened. Do not overcook.

Whisk well. Add lemon juice; stir and refrigerate. Sauce will thicken during the chilling time. Serve cold.

Makes about 1 cup.

"<u>Help</u>" - For a delicious orange sauce, substitute grated orange rind and 1/4 cup orange juice for lemon rind and juice.

MALTAISE SAUCE

"Try this delicate orange butter sauce over asparagus or broccoli."

3 egg yolks, beaten
3 tablespoons freshly squeezed orange juice
1/2 teaspoon finely grated orange rind
dash cayenne
dash white pepper
1/4 teaspoon salt
1/2 cup butter

Combine egg yolks, orange juice, orange rind, cayenne and white pepper in a small, glass mixing bowl; set aside.

Heat butter for 45 seconds or until just bubbling around edges. Slowly add butter to egg yolk mixture, beating constantly with wire whisk. Microwave 15 seconds; immediately whisk sauce for 15 seconds. Microwave 15 seconds more; immediately whisk sauce for 15 seconds or more. Microwave 15 seconds more; immediately whisk about 30 seconds.

If sauce has thickened to the consistency of heavy cream, stir in salt and serve. If sauce needs to thicken more, repeat last step above.

Makes about 3/4 cup.

"Help" - To prevent curdling, do not overcook; be sure to follow directions for stirring and whisking very carefully. If sauce starts to cook rapidly around edges in the last 2 microwaving steps, immediately whisk and place bowl in a bowl of cold water; continue beating.

If sauce curdles, beat in 1 to 2 tablespoons of cream, or add slowly to a fresh egg yolk, whisking constantly.

For Hollandaise Sauce, substitute 4 ½ teaspoons of lemon juice for orange juice and grated orange rind.

VANILLA SAUCE

"This is essential over Swedish Apple Dessert, but do try it on other desserts too."

1/4 cup sugar
1 tablespoon cornstarch
1/4 teaspoon salt
3 egg yolks
1 cup milk
1 cup light cream
1 teaspoon vanilla

Combine sugar, cornstarch and salt in a 1 quart glass measure. Add egg yolks, milk and cream; beating well with a wire whisk.

Microwave 3½ minutes; stir very well with a metal spoon.

Microwave 1 minute; stir very well.

Microwave 30 to 90 seconds more, stirring very well every 30 seconds. Cook until mixture thickens and coats metal spoon. Do not overcook.

Add vanilla and stir well. Immediately pour into a clean dish and refrigerate. Chill well before serving.

Makes 2½ cups.

"Help" - Add a bit of almond extract to this sauce and serve over drained warm poached peach slices or halves.

Vegetables

ASPARAGUS SPEARS WITH TOMATOES AND CHEESE

"Another attractive and delicious-tasting vegetable dish again proves that microwaved vegetables are superior."

8 small fresh tomatoes or 8 small whole
   canned tomatoes
2 pounds fresh asparagus
1/2 cup hot tap water
salt and freshly grated pepper
1/2 to 3/4 cup grated sharp cheddar cheese

Peel fresh tomatoes, quarter and let stand in colander to drain. If using canned tomatoes, quarter and let stand in colander to drain.

Snap off tough ends of asparagus and discard. Wash asparagus well. Hold tips of asparagus evenly together and cut off bottom ends so asparagus spears are 5 inches long. (Save ends; slice and cook for another meal.)

With string, tie asparagus together in a bunch.

In a deep 2-quart glass bowl or measure, microwave water, covered, until boiling - about 1 to 1½ minutes.

Add tied asparagus with stem ends down. Cover with plastic wrap and microwave about 6 minutes or until almost tender.

Place tomatoes in small glass bowl and microwave about 2 minutes or until very hot.

(continued)

ASPARAGUS SPEARS WITH TOMATOES AND CHEESE
(continued)

Working quickly, carefully remove plastic wrap from asparagus, cut string and arrange asparagus on small oval serving platter. Sprinkle with salt and pepper. Arrange tomatoes over top, leaving tips and bottoms of asparagus showing. Sprinkle with cheese. Cover tightly and let stand 3 to 5 minutes or until cheese is melted.

Makes 4 to 6 servings.

"Help" - Two packages (10 ounces each) frozen asparagus spears may be used. Cook until almost tender.

Asparagus may be cooked in a 6 x 8 inch glass baking dish. Arrange asparagus so tips are to center and stalk end (which takes longer to cook) are to outside edges.

For even cooking, asparagus spears should be about the same thickness. If not, thicker stalk ends may be slit.

For an entirely different-tasting asparagus dish, be sure to try asparagus spears with Maltaise Sauce (page 56). To serve, insert hot cooked asparagus spears into unpeeled orange rounds. Arrange spoke-fashion on a large round serving plate with a container of Maltaise Sauce in center.

This same tomato-cheese combination is very good with frozen artichoke hearts. Microwave 2 packages (10 ounces each) artichoke hearts in a covered glass casserole until almost tender. Add drained tomatoes and microwave until very hot. Season and sprinkle with grated cheese. Let stand, covered, to melt cheese. Makes 6 to 8 servings.

ESCALLOPED SPINACH CASSEROLE

"Canned cream soup is used for extra convenience in this flavorful vegetable or main dish."

3 tablespoons butter
1/4 pound small mushrooms, sliced
2 packages (10 ounces each) frozen chopped spinach, thawed and well-drained
4 eggs, slightly beaten
1 can (10 oz.) condensed cream of onion soup
1/4 cup fine dry bread crumbs
1/2 teaspoon lemon juice
2 tablespoons grated Parmesan cheese
dash pepper
1/8 teaspoon salt

Put butter and mushrooms in medium glass bowl; microwave 2 minutes.

Stir in remaining ingredients. Pour into a buttered 10-inch glass quiche dish, shallow glass casserole or a 10 x 7 inch glass dish. Microwave 6 minutes.

Stir cooked outside edges to center and rotate dish. Microwave 4 to 6 minutes more or until knife inserted near center comes out clean. Cover and let stand 5 minutes.

Makes 8 to 10 servings as a vegetable or 6 to 8 servings as a main dish.

"Help" - About 2 pounds fresh spinach (3 cups cooked, chopped and well-drained) may be used. About 1 3/4 pound fresh broccoli (3½ cups cooked, chopped and well-drained) or 2 packages (10 ounces each) frozen, chopped broccoli, thawed and well-drained may be substituted for the spinach.

Try using a 6-cup microwave-safe ring mold. Allow about 1 minute less cooking time. Let stand 5 minutes and unmold onto serving plate--lovely!

GREEN BEANS WITH QUICK MUSTARD SAUCE

"Try this tangy sauce on broccoli too."

1 pound fresh young uniform-size green beans
1 ½ ounces (half of a 3-ounce package) cream cheese
2 tablespoons milk
1/4 teaspoon Dijon mustard
salt and pepper

Wash beans; drain. Trim ends and place in a 1½ quart glass casserole. Microwave, covered, for 8 to 12 minutes or until desired doneness, rearranging once. Let stand, covered for 3 minutes.

In 1-cup glass measure, microwave cream cheese and milk for 15 seconds; stir well.

Stir in mustard and microwave 15 seconds or until hot.

Drain beans and arrange attracively in casserole or on serving plate. Sprinkle lightly with salt and pepper. Serve with sauce

Makes 4 to 5 servings.

"Help" - Be sure not to overcook the beans. The beans must be cooked only to a slightly crisp-tender stage. It is impossible to microwave fresh beans to a soft stage as we may be used to doing conventionally - they would only toughen in the microwave.

ITALIAN VEGETABLE MEDLEY

"Here's an eye-appealing, fresh-tasting, crunchy medley of vegetables cooked in a mild Italian marinade."

3 cups separated broccoli flowerettes (3/4 to 1 inch in diameter)
1 ½ cups separated cauliflower flowerettes (3/4 to 1 inch in diameter)
1 cup thinly sliced carrots (in rounds)
1 tablespoon chopped sweet red pepper or pimento
3/4 cup Italian Marinade
12 to 15 whole pitted ripe olives

Italian Marinade:

In blender container, combine 3/4 cup salad oil, 1/3 cup white vinegar, 1 clove garlic (quartered), 1 tablespoon coarsly chopped onion, 1/2 teaspoon salt, 1/8 teaspoon dried rosemary, 1/8 teaspoon dried basil, 1/4 teaspoon dried oregano and dash cayenne. Blend until garlic and onion are liquified. Makes about 1 cup.

Arrange vegetables in a 9-inch glass quiche dish or 10-inch glass pie plate; placing broccoli, flower side up, around outside; then cauliflower, flower side up; and finally carrots in center. Scatter red pepper over top.

Spoon 3/4 cup Italian Marinade evenly over all vegetables.

Cover with plastic wrap. Microwave 4 minutes. Rotate dish if necessary.

Carefully remove plastic wrap and arrange the ripe olives attractively over the other vegetables.

(continued)

ITALIAN VEGETABLE MEDLEY (continued)

Serve immediately as a hot vegetable; cool uncovered, and serve at room temperature as a first course; or refrigerate and serve cold as a salad.

Makes 4 to 6 servings.

"Help" - Cut broccoli and cauliflower in uniform size pieces.

Have all ingredients at about the same temperature (ex.-all from refrigerator or all at room temperature).

If serving this as a hot vegetable, make marinade ahead so flavors can blend.

Remove plastic wrap right after cooking to preserve the bright, green color of the broccoli.

To use remaining broccoli, cauliflower stems, and Italian Marinade, cut stems in ½ inch thick slices and place in a 1-quart glass casserole. Pour Italian Marinade over them; cover. Microwave 2½ to 3½ minutes (for about 2 cups of vegetables). Stems may also be cooked in butter and the remaining Italian Marinade used as a salad dressing.

PARMESAN BROCCOLI AND BACON

"Parmesan cheese and bacon adds a new taste to a very versatile vegetable."

1 ½ pounds fresh broccoli
6 to 8 slices bacon
1/4 cup freshly grated parmesan cheese
white pepper
1/8 teaspoon dried basil, crushed

Wash broccoli; cut into spears about 5 inches long. If stalks are more than 1-inch in diameter, split stalk all the way through the head. Set aside.

Allow ½ slice bacon for each broccoli spear. Layer bacon between paper towels. Microwave bacon until just half cooked, 3-4 minutes, depending on number of slices used. Cut each slice in half.

Wrap half piece of bacon around each broccoli stalk. Lay broccoli in 11 x 7 inch glass baking dish so stalks are to outside and heads to center of dish. Cover with plastic wrap. Microwave 7 to 9 minutes or until the broccoli is just about tender.

Carefully lift plastic wrap; sprinkle broccoli with cheese, pepper and basil. Cover and let stand about 5 minutes to finish cooking.

Makes 4 to 6 servings.

"Help" - Save trimmings from broccoli for another meal. Slice stalks ¼ inch thick diagonally (peel, if outside is tough). Cut flowerettes in ½ inch pieces. Put stalks and several slices of diced bacon in a dish. Cover and microwave until broccoli turns bright green; stir several times. Stir in flowerettes and microwave until they turn bright green. Stir in a few tablespoons of dry, white wine and microwave 15 to 30 seconds just to heat. Add freshly grated black pepper and serve. Broccoli should be crisp-tender.

STUFFED POTATOES SUPREME

"Tiny pieces of pink shrimp add eye and taste appeal to these elegant stuffed potatoes."

4 medium baking potatoes
1/3 cup tiny cooked shrimp
1/4 cup butter
1/2 cup dairy sour cream
1/8 teaspoon white pepper
1/2 teaspoon salt
1/2 teaspoon Dijon mustard
2 tablespoons minced chives
minced chives for garnish

Scrub potatoes and pierce skin 2 times with a fork. Arrange potatoes in a circle on paper towels and microwave 13 to 15 minutes or until potatoes begin to feel soft. Turn potatoes over half-way through cooking period. Let stand, covered, for 5 minutes until completely baked.

Reserve 8 shrimp for garnish; cut remaining shrimp in halves.

Cut potatoes in half lengthwise. Carefully scoop out potatoe pulp. Set shells aside. Mash potatoe pulp until soft and free from lumps. Stir in butter, sour cream, white pepper, salt, mustard and chives. Gently stir in shrimp.

Fill potatoe shells, placing on serving plate. Garnish with minced chives and one whole shrimp. Immediately microwave 3 minutes or until hot and serve; or refrigerate or freeze. For refrigerated potatoes, microwave about 5 minutes. For frozen potatoes, microwave about 15 minutes or until hot. (Do not thaw first.) Makes 4 large or 8 small servings.

"Help" - One can (4½ ounces) of tiny shrimp, drained, can be used. For frozen stuffed potatoes, freeze shrimp separately and garnish towards the end of the 15 minute microwave time.

Joyce Battcher is a home economist, teacher, demonstrator, writer of a weekly newspaper column, author and a member of the International Microwave Power Institute/Cooking Appliance Section.

She received her degree in foods from the University of Minnesota. Her expertise has inspired many adult students in the area of foods, where she has taught numerous classes. Her many talents and enjoyment of people have been evident in her work as Coordinator of Volunteer Services for County Social Service departments, Advisor to Home Economist Extension Agents in Laos, and as Home Economist for two gas companies.

This booklet, together with her lesson plan, has been sold nationally and internationally.

****

Arlene Hedahl Hamernik is a Free Lance Home Economist specializing in Microwave Consulting. She has taught and coordinated microwave cooking classes for adults throughout the St. Paul and Minneapolis suburban area for the past 6½ years. Her lesson plan is being used in numerous states and abroad. Her consulting work has also included demonstrating, customer information resource and conducting training sessions for Home Economists, service agents, and demonstrators for manufacturers and national distributors. She is also a member of the National Home Economics Association and the International Micowave Power Institute. In May, 1977, she spoke on "Educating the Microwave Oven User" at the International Microwave Symposium.

Available from <u>Microwave "Helps"</u>:

<u>MICROWAVING WITH A GOURMET FLAIR</u> by Joyce Battcher.   Recipe Booklet $2.00
  18 page lesson plan + Recipe booklet 7.00

<u>101 MICROWAVE FAVORITES</u> + 4 by Arlene Hamernik. Includes over 110 helpful tips and special sections of Sharing Concerns and Have You Tried...   Spiral $2.95

<u>BASIC MICROWAVE COOKING LESSON PLAN</u> - 55 pages with information and recipes for four classes each 2½ hours long. Saves many hours of planning for teachers. By Arlene $10.00

<u>FOOD PROCESSOR RECIPES FOR CONVENTIONAL AND MICROWAVE COOKING</u> by Sharon Dlugosch and Joyce Battcher.   Spiral $3.25

<u>FOLDING TABLE NAPKINS</u>: A New Look at a Traditional Craft by Sharon Dlugosch. Inquire about lesson plan.   Spiral $3.50

<u>YES YOU CAN TEACH</u> - For anyone who wants to teach anything by Florence Nelson.
              58 page spiral $5.00

<u>THE BEST OF HELPFUL HINTS</u> - A collection of over 1000 hints for cooking, painting, cleaning, gardening, sewing, repairing, washing, etc..   Spiral $3.95

Wear-ever 6-cup capacity plastic <u>RING MOLD</u> (size recommended in some recipes in this booklet). $4.75

TAX: Minnesota residents add 4%.

SHIPPING: $ .65 for one or two items.
          1.00 for three or four items.

Order from: MICROWAVE "HELPS"
            P.O. Box 32223
            Minneapolis, Minnesota 55432